DREAMS TO ASHES

The 1871 Los Angeles Chinatown Massacre

LIVIA BLACKBURNE ··· NICOLE XU

CAROLRHODA BOOKS
Minneapolis

WHAT SPARKS A FIRE
IN A YOUNG CALIFORNIA CITY?

What ignites those flashes in time
that force humankind to pause?

To question?

To mourn and reflect?

This story culminates in 1871 Los Angeles,
but it started an ocean away.

It started in China decades earlier. Years of war, natural disasters, and meddling from foreign governments had made life difficult for those who lived there.

It started with thousands of young men who rolled up their beds, packed belongings into baskets, and walked away from their villages in search of a better life.

From across the Pacific, they'd heard news of California, the land of the Gold Mountain. A rich land with treasure for all who came.

So they borrowed money for the two-month boat passage and pledged to pay it back with interest. They traveled to a country with foreign customs and an alien tongue. They planned to work hard and send money home to their families. Once they made their fortune, they would return to China.

But gold proved elusive on Gold Mountain.

So these travelers chased their fortune in other ways, as doctors and launderers, cooks and gangsters. Vegetable peddlers and houseboys.

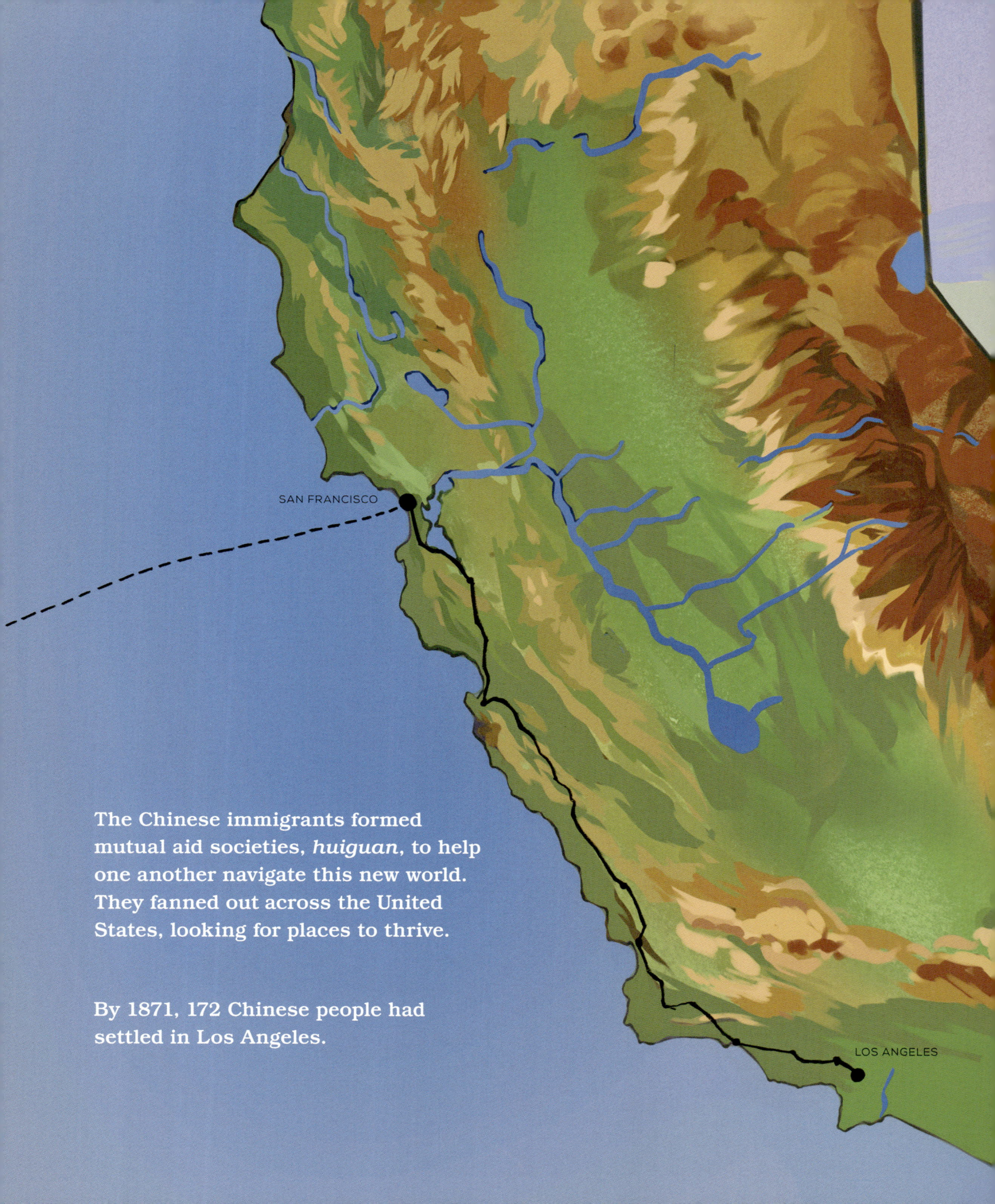

It was a small city of hot, dusty roads and green-gold citrus trees. Perfumed gardens and rotting gutters. Squat adobe homes and taller brick buildings. Violence was common. Brawls frequently broke out, and many people took the law into their own hands.

English-speaking farmers were moving in, replacing Spanish-speaking Californios and turning their cattle ranches into fruit orchards.

People from the Gabrielino Tongva, Serrano, Kizh, Gabrielino-Shoshone, and Tataviam Nations also lived and worked in the city. Yet significant numbers of them had been killed by disease, genocide, and forced labor for the Spanish colonial missions.

The Chinese immigrants lived their lives in this growing, changing city.

In an old adobe apartment building, Dr. Gene Tong treated patients of all backgrounds with Chinese and Western medicine. At home, he and his wife played with their pet poodle.

Newly arrived from San Francisco, Tong Won performed music at lively gatherings. And Wing Chee cooked elaborate Chinese banquets for his countrymen.

Gene Tong, Tong Won, Wing Chee, and the others lived in a land that grew to resent their presence. The California legislature passed a law preventing Chinese people from testifying against white people in a court of law. Newspapers accused them of taking jobs from white citizens. Articles called Chinese immigrants inferior and immoral. Degraded and disgusting. Aliens. Rats. Barbarians.

Hateful words built up like dry kindling on a hot day. The Chinese immigrants became less than human in the eyes of their neighbors.

Physical attacks against Chinese people increased throughout the late 1860s. All the while, hateful messages continued.

The kindling continued to build. Until . . .

What ignites an inferno?

A feud between two *huiguan* became increasingly tense and led to a gunfight on October 24, 1871. The fighters shot a police officer, then killed another man who rushed to his aid.

A spark.

Reports and rumors spread like flames. People on the streets called for revenge, blaming anyone with a Chinese name. The shooting had taken place in a large building with shops and apartments, a complex where many Chinese residents lived and worked. Now a mob formed and surrounded it. They didn't know that most of the gunfighters had already fled, leaving their unsuspecting Chinese neighbors behind.

The sheriff and city marshal deputized bystanders to shoot any Chinese people attempting to escape. But the mob grew impatient with simply waiting. As they surged toward violence, some lawmen tried to pull Chinese people from the mob and escort them to safety. Others looked the other way. The mayor came and silently left.

What kinds of people bring about humanity's greatest horrors?

Criminals and drifters?

Or upstanding citizens?

Eighteen Chinese men killed.

Gene Tong, Tong Won, Wing Chee, and fifteen others, only one of whom had been in the original gunfight.

Walls pitted,
rooftops torn open.
Homes and stores in tatters.

A grief-stricken Chinese community buried the victims in a section of the cemetery meant for outcasts. The survivors wondered whether it was safe to stay.

A nation left horrified. Newspapers from Philadelphia to Albany condemned the violence. In California, papers that had attacked and dehumanized the Chinese for years mourned the massacre with no mention of the role they might have played.

In the light of day, a country hoped for justice. Chinese people in Los Angeles filed lawsuits against the city, and Chinese communities in other cities sent aid.

Of a mob of five hundred, twenty-five men were charged in the attack. Ten stood trial. No Chinese witnesses were allowed to testify.

Eight men were convicted, but the California Supreme Court overturned their sentences a year later. The court's reason? A legal technicality. The original charges failed to claim that the victim had been murdered.

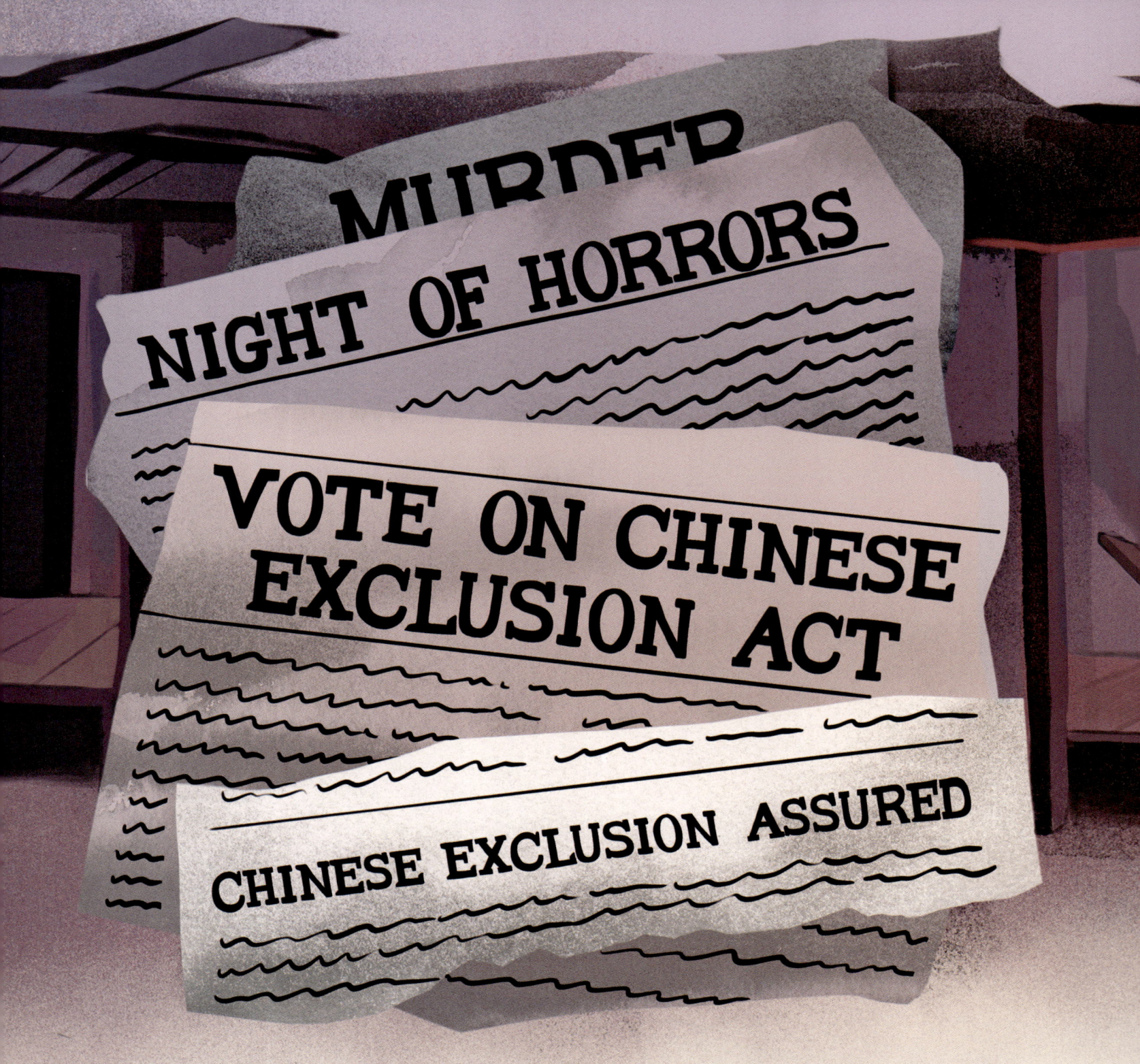

The massacre faded from memory. Newspapers returned to slandering the Chinese. Around the country, attacks continued. Fresno, Pasadena, and Riverside, California, forced Chinese residents to leave. White miners in Rock Springs, Wyoming, killed twenty-eight Chinese miners.

The hatred toward Chinese immigrants was not limited to the West. In 1882, Congress passed the Chinese Exclusion Act, which banned Chinese laborers from immigrating to the United States. Even after the ban was repealed in 1943, the government placed strict limits on immigration from China until 1968.

But Chinese Americans kept living their lives. In Los Angeles, they moved back into Chinatown after the massacre and restarted businesses. Across the country, they hired lawyers and looked for ways to fight unjust laws. They fought for dignity. They continued to strive for their dreams.

How does a country learn from the past?

By remembering. By writing the dark stories back into history books. By shining a light on the consequences of hate and working to keep those fires from sparking again.

By embracing change. By loving those who dream of a better life and affirming the humanity of all. By stepping forward.

Into hope.

HISTORICAL NOTE

In the 1870s, Los Angeles was a small frontier town. While the area boasted pleasant weather and lush orchards, the city itself was run-down, haphazardly built, and lacking in sanitation and basic city services. The city was marked by frequent violence and law enforcement was scarce, so people often took the law into their own hands.

Most members of the city's tiny Chinese community were young men from southern China. After gold was discovered in California in the 1840s, a steady flow of Chinese men began arriving to seek their fortune. Unlike European immigrants who came to the United States with the expectation of staying permanently, the vast majority of Chinese immigrants at the time planned to stay only until they saved enough money to comfortably live out the rest of their lives in China.

The 1860s and 1870s saw an increase in anti-Chinese prejudice across California. Newspapers printed harshly worded editorials, and random acts of violence against Chinese individuals increased. It was against this backdrop that the Los Angeles Chinatown Massacre occurred.

The inciting incident was a feud between two rival Chinese organizations over the kidnapping of a woman named Yut Ho. As tensions escalated, one party brought in professional Chinese gunmen from out of town. A gunfight erupted in a dilapidated building known as the Coronel Adobe. Jesús Bilderrain, a law enforcement officer who attempted to intervene, was shot, and a rancher named Robert Thompson was killed when he rushed into the fray.

Things disintegrated rapidly after that. Within hours, a mob of five hundred had gathered around the Coronel Adobe, clamoring for Chinese blood. Local law enforcement chose to prioritize attempting to capture the criminals over protecting the many Chinese people who lived and worked in the Coronel Adobe. They recruited bystanders, including men known to have violent histories, to surround the building and shoot anyone who attempted to escape.

It didn't work. The Chinese gunfighters who'd participated in the original gunfight had already fled, leaving their innocent countrymen to the mob. Eventually, the crowd became restless and moved in on the trapped Chinese people inside the building. Thirty minutes later, eighteen men were killed, which amounted to 10 percent of the Los Angeles Chinese population.

Initial newspaper reports about the massacre were quick to blame "the dregs of society" for the violence, but the truth was that Angelenos from all backgrounds participated that night. Witnesses reported seeing a city councilman and a future mayor among the mob.

As news of the massacre spread across the nation, it was met with widespread outrage and horror, as well as calls for justice. However, lawyers had trouble charging people with the crimes. Many factors contributed to this. The darkness and the fact that so many people had been involved made it difficult to connect any individual person to a specific crime. Witnesses were also reluctant to testify, possibly out of fear for their safety. Finally, legal restrictions barred Chinese witnesses from testifying in court.

In the end, twenty-five men were indicted. Eight of them were found guilty of manslaughter

Los Angeles's first Chinatown developed in the 1860s around Calle de Los Negros (*shown here*). The Coronel Adobe, where the massacre took place, was located on this street.

Chinese immigrants brought their festivals and traditions with them to California. In this photograph from 1899, several men parade a paper dragon down a Los Angeles road. Dragon dances are often performed as part of Chinese New Year celebrations.

(the unlawful killing of a person without planning or meaning to do so) and given short prison sentences ranging from two to six years. However, the California Supreme Court overturned the convictions a year later because of a technical legal error: the original charges failed to state that the murder victim had actually been murdered. The men were released.

Unfortunately, the Los Angeles Chinatown Massacre did little to curb racism in its aftermath. Anti-Chinese sentiment increased in the following years, and Chinese immigrants continued to face violence from their surrounding communities. In 1882, Congress passed the Chinese Exclusion Act, banning Chinese laborers from entering the United States. The act also excluded Chinese immigrants from becoming US citizens. Congress continued to strictly limit Chinese immigration well into the twentieth century.

The massacre itself quickly faded from memory. Several local newspapers didn't even mention it in year-end news roundups. Over time, the tragedy was largely left out of history books and classes.

The US government eventually removed its ban on Chinese immigrants in the mid-twentieth century, and Asian Americans have since made significant inroads integrating into American society. However, racially motivated violence, including violence against Asian Americans, stubbornly persists in the US. Most recently, there was a marked uptick in anti-Asian hate crimes in the wake of the COVID-19 epidemic.

Recently, coverage by historians and journalists have brought the LA massacre back into the public consciousness. In 2021, the city of Los Angeles convened a committee to plan a memorial commemorating this dark chapter in California's history and to draw attention to the tragic consequences of racial prejudice. The committee selected a design by Sze Tsung Nicolás Leong and Judy Chui-Hua Chung in 2023, with a goal of completing the memorial by 2026.

SELECTED BIBLIOGRAPHY

"Chinese Exclusion Act, 1882." National Archives. January 17, 2023. https://www.archives.gov/milestone-documents/chinese-exclusion-act.

Grad, Shelby. "The Racist Massacre That Killed 10% of L.A.'s Chinese Population and Brought Shame to the City." *Los Angeles Times*, March 18, 2021. https://www.latimes.com/california/story/2021-03-18/reflecting-los-angeles-chinatown-massacre-after-atlanta-shootings.

Huang, Josie. "Here's the Winning Design for LA's Memorial to the 1871 Chinese Massacre." LAist, May 4, 2023. https://laist.com/news/la-history/chinese-massacre-1871-memorial-winning-design.

"Immigration and Relocation in U.S. History: Chinese." Library of Congress. Accessed August 21, 2024. https://www.loc.gov/classroom-materials/immigration/chinese/.

Johnson, John, Jr. "How Los Angeles Covered Up the Massacre of 17 Chinese." *LA Weekly*, March 10, 2011. https://www.laweekly.com/how-los-angeles-covered-up-the-massacre-of-17-chinese/.

Lee, Erika. *The Making of Asian America: A History*. New York: Simon & Schuster, 2016.

Leewong, Cameron, dir. *Buried History: Retracing the Chinese Massacre of 1871*. Directed by Chinese American Museum, Los Angeles, 2021.

Rasmussen, Cecilia. "A Forgotten Hero from a Night of Disgrace." *Los Angeles Times*, May 16, 1999. https://www.latimes.com/archives/la-xpm-1999-may-16-me-37851-story.html.

Roman, James. *Chronicles of Old Los Angeles: Exploring the Devilish History of the City of the Angels*. Los Angeles: Museyon, 2015.

Wallace, Kelly. "Forgotten Los Angeles History: The Chinese Massacre of 1871." Los Angeles Public Library, May 19, 2017. https://www.lapl.org/collections-resources/blogs/lapl/chinese-massacre-1871.

Woo, Michael. "After 150 Years, Is L.A. Ready to Remember the Chinese Massacre?" Zocálo Public Square, October 24, 2021. https://www.zocalopublicsquare.org/2021/10/24/remember-1871-chinatown-massacre-los-angeles/ideas/essay/.

Yam, Kimmy. "Anti-Asian Hate Crimes Increased 339 Percent Nationwide Last Year, Report Says." NBC News, January 31, 2022. https://www.nbcnews.com/news/asian-america/anti-asian-hate-crimes-increased-339-percent-nationwide-last-year-repo-rcna14282.

Zesch, Scott. *The Chinatown War: Chinese Los Angeles and the Massacre of 1871*. New York: Oxford University Press, 2012.

In memory of the eighteen —L.B.

For my mom —N.X.

Grateful acknowledgment to Hao Huang 黄俊豪, Bessie and Cecil Frankel Endowed Chair in Music, Scripps College, and host and producer of the *Blood on Gold Mountain* podcast, for reviewing the text and illustrations for accuracy.

Quotation source: "the dregs of society": Scott Zesch, *The Chinatown War: Chinese Los Angeles and the Massacre of 1871* (New York: Oxford University Press, 2012), 169.

Text copyright © 2025 by Livia Blackburne
Illustrations copyright © 2025 by Nicole Xu

All rights reserved. International copyright secured. No part of this book may be reproduced, stored in a retrieval system, or transmitted in any form or by any means—electronic, mechanical, photocopying, recording, or otherwise—without the prior written permission of Lerner Publishing Group, Inc., except for the inclusion of brief quotations in an acknowledged review.

Carolrhoda Books®
An imprint of Lerner Publishing Group, Inc.
241 First Avenue North
Minneapolis, MN 55401 USA

For reading levels and more information, look up this title at www.lernerbooks.com.

Photo credits: Los Angeles Public Library via Wikimedia Commons PD, p. 38; Courtesy of the Workman and Temple Family Homestead Museum, City of Industry, California, p. 39.

Designed by Danielle Carnito.
Main body text set in ITC Bookman Std. Typeface provided by Adobe Systems.
The illustrations in this book were created with ink and Photoshop.

Library of Congress Cataloging-in-Publication Data

Names: Blackburne, Livia, author. | Xu, Nicole, 1994– illustrator.
Title: Dreams to ashes : the 1871 Los Angeles Chinatown Massacre / Livia Blackburne ; [illustrated by] Nicole Xu.
Other titles: 1871 Los Angeles Chinatown Massacre
Description: Minneapolis : Carolrhoda Books, [2025] | Includes bibliographical references. | Audience: Ages 7–11 | Audience: Grades 2–3 | Summary: "A powerful nonfiction picture book about the history of Chinese immigration to the West Coast, presented through the lens of the 1871 Los Angeles Chinatown Massacre. An essential account that offers both heartbreak and hope" —Provided by publisher.
Identifiers: LCCN 2024020217 (print) | LCCN 2024020218 (ebook) | ISBN 9798765627228 (library binding) | ISBN 9798765650981 (epub)
Subjects: LCSH: Los Angeles Massacre, Los Angeles, Calif., 1871—Juvenile literature. | Chinese Americans—California—Los Angeles—History—19th century—Juvenile literature. | Chinese Americans—Crimes against—California—Los Angeles—History—19th century—Juvenile literature. | Race riots—California—Los Angeles—History—19th century—Juvenile literature. | Los Angeles (Calif.)—Ethnic relations—History—19th century—Juvenile literature. | Los Angeles (Calif.)—History—19th century—Juvenile literature.
Classification: LCC F869.L86 C4526 2025 (print) | LCC F869.L86 (ebook) | DDC 305.895/107949409034—dc23/eng/20240510

LC record available at https://lccn.loc.gov/2024020217
LC ebook record available at https://lccn.loc.gov/2024020218

Manufactured in the United States of America
1-1010939-52104-9/17/2024